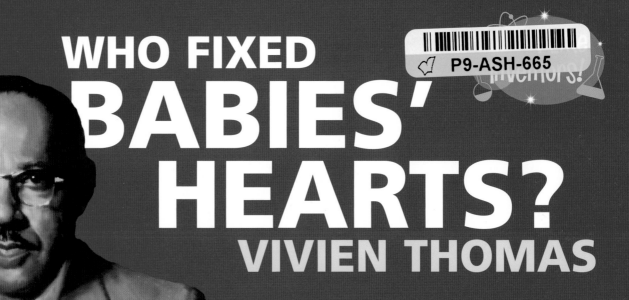

WHO FIXED BABIES' HEARTS?

VIVIEN THOMAS

Sara L. Latta

Enslow Elementary
an imprint of
Enslow Publishers, Inc.
40 Industrial Road
Box 398
Berkeley Heights, NJ 07922
USA
http://www.enslow.com

CONTENTS

A NEW WAY TO SAVE LIVES   5

DREAMS OF BEING A DOCTOR   6

LEARNING ON THE JOB   9

A HEART MYSTERY   10

A NEW LIFE IN MARYLAND   13

BLUE BABIES   14

THOMAS'S INVENTION   17

A BLUE BABY TURNS PINK   18

ACTIVITY: LISTEN TO YOUR HEART   20

LEARN MORE: BOOKS   22

                   WEB SITES   23

INDEX   24

WORDS TO KNOW

blood—The red liquid that flows through the body. It carries oxygen and other things that the organs need to work.

invent—To think of something for the first time or find a new way of doing something.

operation—Cutting into a person to fix a medical problem.

vessel—A tube that carries blood throughout the body.

A NEW WAY TO SAVE LIVES

Cookie was very sick. Her heart did not work well. Children with Cookie's problem did not live very long. Vivien Thomas invented a way to fix the little girl's heart. He saved the life of Cookie and other children like her.

DREAMS OF BEING
A DOCTOR

Thomas wanted to be a doctor. He lived in a time when black people were not treated fairly. But a black doctor could help other black people. It took money to learn how to become a doctor. Thomas, like many others in this hard time, did not have enough money.

Vivien Thomas lived from 1910 to 1985. He grew up in Nashville, Tennessee.

PETER'S MISSION

The 1930s were hard times. Here, people with no jobs wait in line for free food in New York City.

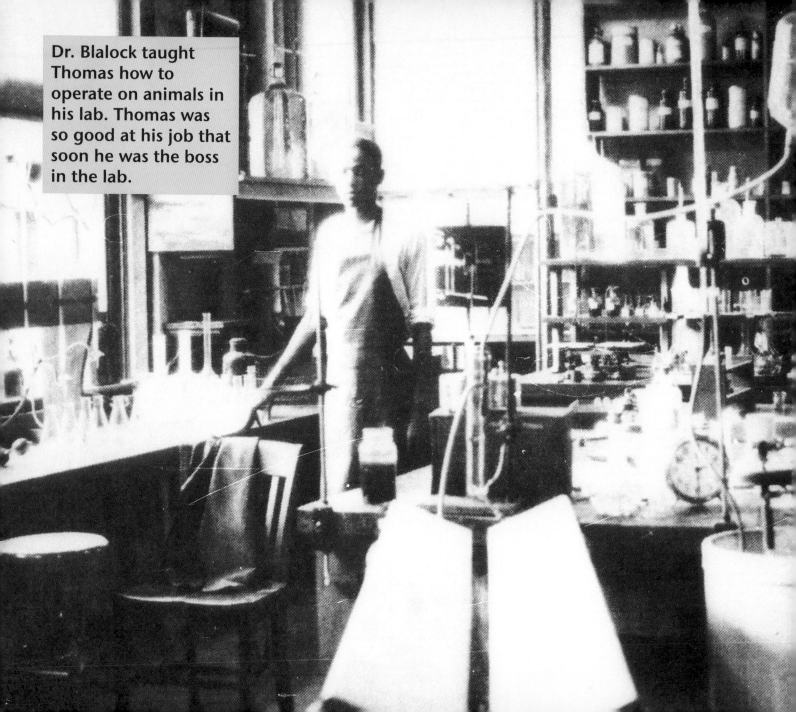

Dr. Blalock taught Thomas how to operate on animals in his lab. Thomas was so good at his job that soon he was the boss in the lab.

LEARNING
ON THE JOB

Thomas found a job helping a doctor. His name was Alfred Blalock. Dr. Blalock had a lab. He studied animals. The men in the lab wanted to know how their bodies worked. What they learned would help them treat sick people.

Dr. Alfred Blalock

9

A HEART
MYSTERY

Thomas helped Dr. Blalock solve a mystery. When a person got sick or hurt, sometimes the heart could not get enough **blood** to the rest of the body. Why? No one knew. Working side by side, the men figured it out.

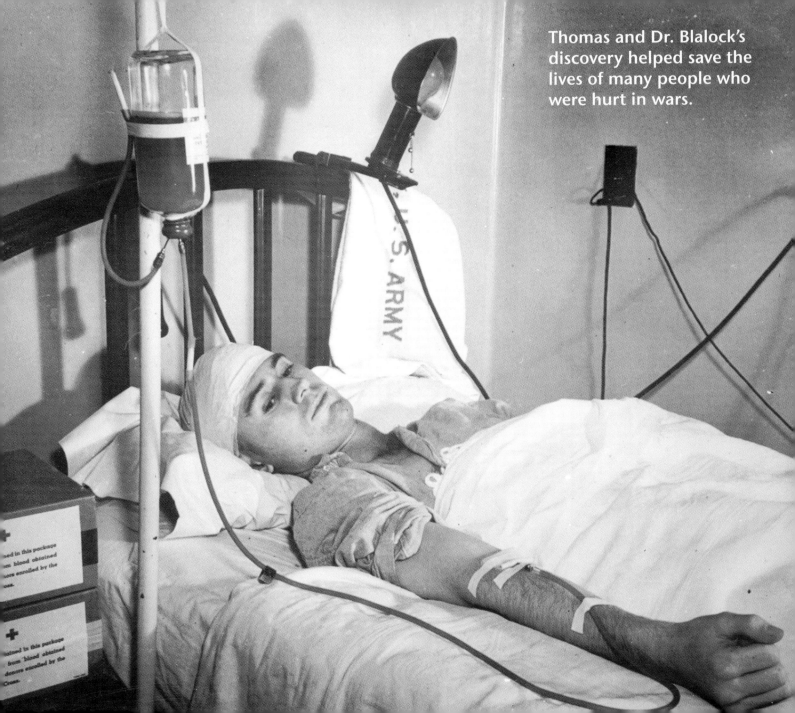

Thomas and Dr. Blalock's discovery helped save the lives of many people who were hurt in wars.

Some white people thought that it was strange for a black man to have such an important job. But they soon saw that he had a special talent in the lab.

THOMAS'S
INVENTION

Dr. Blalock was too busy to solve the problem. He asked Thomas to try. Thomas operated on the animals in the lab. There is a blood vessel that sends blood out into the body. Thomas found a way to connect it to the lungs, too. He made new tools to do the **operation**.

A BLUE BABY TURNS PINK

At last, the men were ready to try the new operation on a baby. Cookie was one of the first babies. Dr. Blalock operated. Thomas watched to help him do it right. When Dr. Blalock finished, Cookie's skin turned pink. She grew up. She was healthy. Thomas and Dr. Blalock saved many more "blue babies."

WEB SITES

The Children's Heart Institute

<http://www.childrensheartinstitute.org>

KidsHealth: Your Heart and Circulatory System

<http://kidshealth.org/kid/htbw/heart.html>

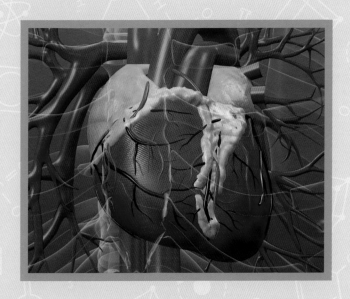

INDEX

B
Blalock, Alfred, 9, 10, 13, 14, 17, 18
blood, 10, 14, 17
blue baby, 14, 18

C
Cookie, 5, 18

H
heart, 5, 10, 14

L
lab, 9, 17

M
Maryland, 13

N
Nashville, 13

O
operation, 17, 18

T
Thomas, Vivien, 5, 6, 9, 10, 13, 14, 17, 18

Library of Congress Cataloging-in-Publication Data
Latta, Sara L.
    Who fixed babies' hearts? Vivien Thomas / Sara L. Latta.
       p. cm. — (I like inventors!)
    Summary: "Read about Vivien Thomas, a man who helped save lives"— Provided by publisher.
    Includes index.
    ISBN 978-0-7660-3963-6
    1. Thomas, Vivien T., 1910-1985—Juvenile literature. 2. Operating room technicians—Maryland—Biography—Juvenile literature. 3. Congenital heart disease—Juvenile literature. I. Title.
    RD32.3.L38 2013
    617.4'12092—dc23
    [B]   2011017690

Future editions:

Paperback ISBN 978-1-4644-0130-5

ePUB ISBN 978-1-4645-1037-3

PDF ISBN 978-1-4646-1037-0

Printed in China
012012 Leo Paper Group, Heshan City, Guangdong, China
10 9 8 7 6 5 4 3 2 1

To Our Readers: We have done our best to make sure all Internet Addresses in this book were active and appropriate when we went to press. However, the author and the publisher have no control over and assume no liability for the material available on those Internet sites or on other Web sites they may link to. Any comments or suggestions can be sent by e-mail to comments@enslow.com or to the address on the back cover.

Photo Credits: © 2011 Photos.com, a division of Getty Images, p. 3 (operation); Courtesy of The Alan Mason Chesney Medical Archives of The Johns Hopkins Medical Institutions, pp. 4, 9, 14, 16, 19; Courtesy of Thomas Family/Spark Media, pp. 6, 12; Enslow Publishers, Inc., p. 20; courtesy the Duke Medical Center Archives, p. 8; © Indiapicture/Alamy, p. 15; Library of Congress, Prints and Photographs, p. 11; National Archives and Records Administration, p. 7; Shutterstock.com, pp. 2, 3 (blood, invent, vessel), 4 (inset), 21, 22, 23, 24; Vivien Thomas by Bob Gee, oil on canvas, courtesy of The Alan Mason Chesney Chesney Medical Archives of The Johns Hopkins Medical Institutions, photo by Aaron Levin, p. 1.

Cover Photo: Courtesy of The Alan Mason Chesney Medical Archives of The Johns Hopkins Medical Institutions (inset); Shutterstock.com.

Series Consultant:
Duncan R. Jamieson, PhD
Professor of History
Ashland University
Ashland, OH

Series Literacy Consultant:
Allan A. De Fina, PhD
Dean, College of Education/Professor of
    Literacy Education
New Jersey City University
Past President of the New Jersey Reading Association